Sounds and Letters Skills

Level K

A Division of The McGraw·Hill Companies

Columbus, Ohio

www.sra4kids.com

SRA/McGraw-Hill

A Division of The McGraw·Hill Companies

Send all inquiries to:
SRA/McGraw-Hill
8787 Orion Place
Columbus, OH 43240-4027

Printed in the United States of America.

ISBN 0-07-571902-9

5 6 7 POH 07 06 05 04 03

Table of Contents

UNIT 1 School • **Lesson 13** *Fine Art*

Directions: Find and circle capital letters A, *B, C, D, E, F,* and *G.*

Name _____ Date _____

Directions: Find and circle small letters a, b, c, d, e, f, and g.

Identifying a–g • Sounds and Letters Skills

Directions: Write small letters *a–h* under the matching capital letters.

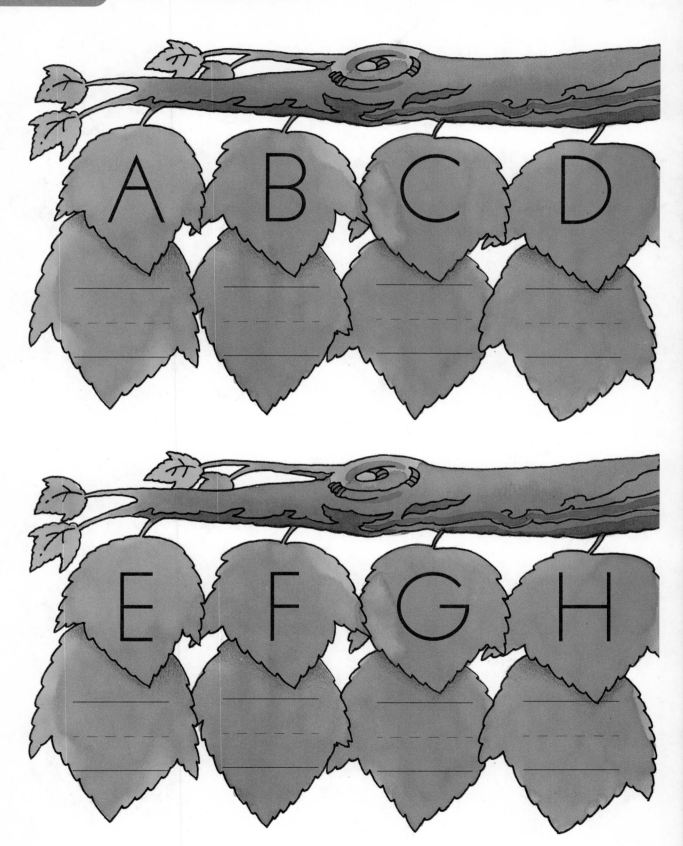

B

D

H

C

I

F

d

b

c

i

h

f

UNIT I   School • **Lesson 19** *Annabelle Swift, Kindergartner*

Directions: Circle the small letter that matches the capital letter.

A   c e a

E   e h l

I   j i l

C   c o e

K   f b k

Directions: Connect the dots, in order from A to L, to complete the picture of the bluebird.

Directions: Practice writing the capital and small forms of the letters *Ll, Mm,* and *Nn*.

L

l

M

m

N

n

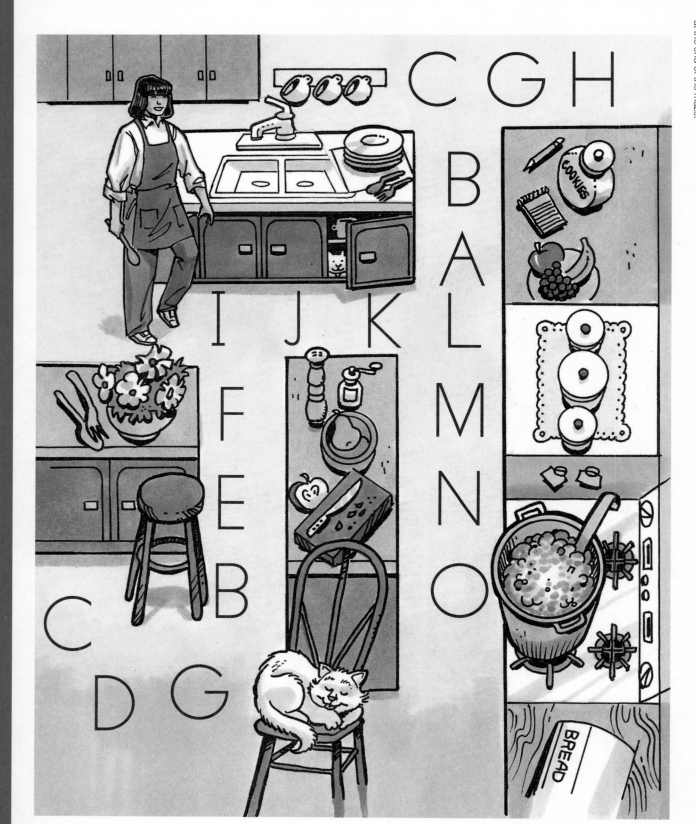

Directions: Connect the capital letters from *I* to *O* to help the chef reach the pot at the end of the maze.

Directions: Circle each capital letter and draw a line to its matching small letter.

M

H T

S H P

F J

h   f   s   m   p   j   t

Sounds and Letters Skills • *Matching Capital and Small Letters*   UNIT 2 • Lesson 9   **9**

Ss

Tt

Directions: Write the capital and small forms of the letters *Ss* and *Tt* and color the flower petals that match the letter in the center of each flower.

UNIT 2   **Shadows • Lesson 12** *The Wolf and His Shadow*

U u
_____

V v
_____

Directions: Write the capital and small forms of the letters *Uu* and *Vv* and color the flower petals that match the letter in the center of each flower.

Directions: Circle each capital letter and draw a line to its small form.

UNIT 2 **Shadows • Lesson 14** *Fine Art*

Directions: Circle each capital letter and draw a line to its small form.

Sounds and Letters Skills • *Matching Capital and Small Letters* UNIT 2 • Lesson 14 **13**

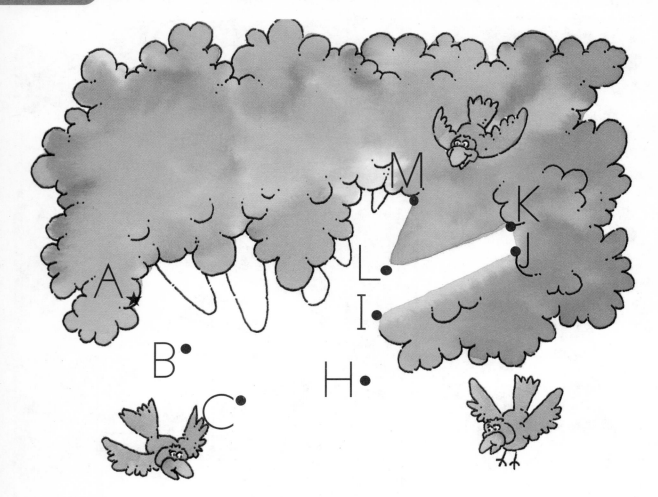

Directions: Connect the dots, in order from A to M, to complete the picture of the elm tree.

Directions: Connect the dots, in order from *N* to *Z*, to complete the picture of the willow tree.

B   b   d

D   b   d

F   f   h

H   h   b

M   n   m

Directions: Circle the small letter that matches each capital letter.

Directions: Circle the small letter that matches each capital letter.

N   m   n

P   p   b

R   r   e

S   c   s

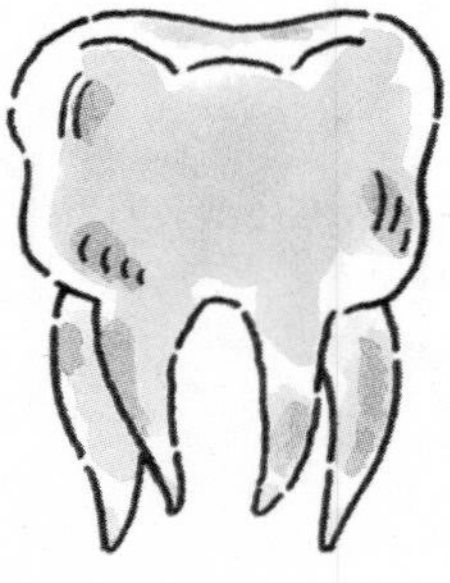

T   l   t

UNIT 3   **Finding Friends • Lesson 9** *The Lonely Prince*

Directions: Circle the word that names the picture.

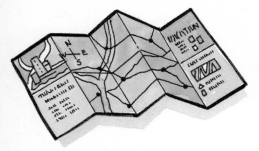

map   apm

ent   net

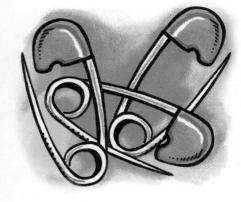

pins   spin

nam   man

Identifying Words • Sounds and Letters Skills

Directions: Circle the word that names the picture.

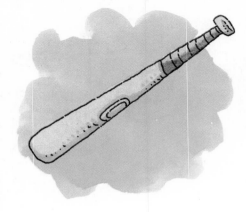

tab   bat

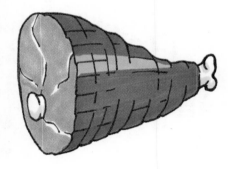

ham   mah

anf   fan

bibs   bisb

UNIT 3 **Finding Friends • Lesson 14** *Fine Art*

Directions: Circle the word that names the picture.

bed   deb

top   pot

hat   tah

spom   mops

UNIT 3   **Finding Friends • Lesson 14** *Fine Art*

Directions: Circle the correct word that names the picture.

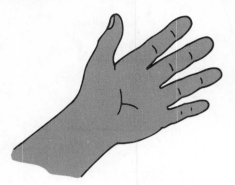 band   hand

 bent   dent

 pond   fond

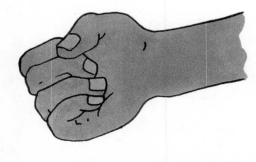 mist   fist

Directions: Fill in the missing letters.

a ___ c

d ___ f g ___

i j ___ l m

___ o p ___ r

s ___ u v ___

___ x ___ z

UNIT 3   Finding Friends • **Lesson 19** *Don't Need Friends*

Directions: Fill in the missing letters.

A B _____

D E F _____ H

I _____ K L _____

N O _____ Q _____

S T U _____ W

_____ Y _____

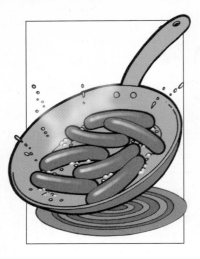

S s

Directions: Write the capital and small forms of the letter Ss. Write the letter s under the picture whose name begins with /s/.

S _____

_____

s _____

_____   _____

_____   _____

UNIT 4 The Wind • **Lesson I** *Unit Introduction*

Directions: Write the letter s under each picture whose name begins with /s/.

_____
- - - - - - - - - - - -
_____

_____
- - - - - - - - - - - -
_____

_____
- - - - - - - - - - - -
_____

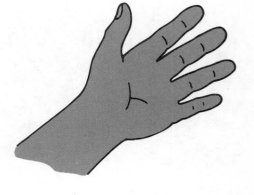

_____
- - - - - - - - - - - -
_____

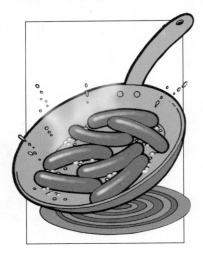

Ss

S _____

s _____

_____   _____

_____   _____

Directions: Write the capital and small forms of the letter Ss. Write the letter s under the picture whose name ends with /s/.

UNIT 4   The Wind • **Lesson 3** *Gilberto and the Wind*

Directions: Write the letter s under each picture whose name ends with /s/.

UNIT 4   The Wind • **Lesson 4** *Gilberto and the Wind*

Directions: Write the capital and small forms of the letter *Mm*. Write the letter *m* under the picture whose name begins with /m/.

Mm

M _____

m _____

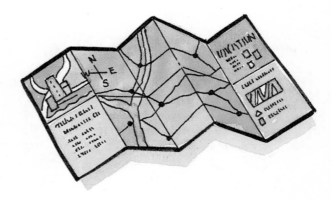

_____

_____

Directions: Write the letter *m* under each picture whose name begins with /m/.

_____

_____

_____

_____

_____

_____

_____

_____

UNIT 4 The Wind • **Lesson 5** *Gilberto and the Wind*

Directions: Write the capital and small forms of the letter *Mm*. Write the letter *m* under the picture whose name ends with /m/.

Mm

M _____

m _____

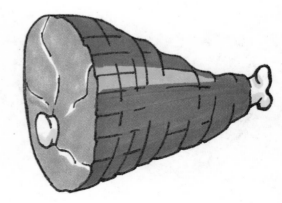

_____   _____

Directions: Write the letter *m* under each picture whose name ends with /m/.

_____

_____

_____

_____

_____

_____

_____

_____

_____

- - - - - - - - - - - - - - -

_____

_____

- - - - - - - - - - - - - - -

_____

Directions: Write *s* under each picture whose name begins with /s/, and write *m* under each picture whose name begins with /m/.

UNIT 4   **The Wind • Lesson 6** *What Happens When Wind Blows?*

Directions: Write s under each picture whose name begins with /s/, and write m under each picture whose name begins with /m/.

_____

- - - - - - - - - - - - - - - - - -

_____

_____

- - - - - - - - - - - - - - - - - -

_____

_____

- - - - - - - - - - - - - - - - - -

_____

_____

- - - - - - - - - - - - - - - - - -

_____

UNIT 4   **The Wind • Lesson 7** *What Happens When Wind Blows?*

Dd

D ——————————————————

d ——————————————————

Directions: Write the capital and small forms of the letter *Dd*. Write the letter *d* under the picture whose name begins with /d/.

———————————————   ———————————————

Directions: Write the letter *d* under each picture whose name begins with /d/.

Dd

D _____

d _____

_____   _____

Directions: Write the capital and small forms of the letter *Dd.* Write the letter *d* under the picture whose name ends with / d / .

Directions: Write the letter *d* under each picture whose name ends with /d/.

_____
- - - - - - - - - -
_____

_____
- - - - - - - - - -
_____

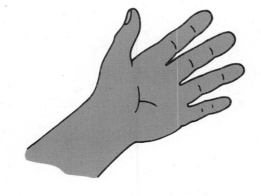

_____
- - - - - - - - - -
_____

_____
- - - - - - - - - -
_____

Sounds and Letters Skills • *Identifying Ending Sound of D*   UNIT 4 • Lesson 8   **37**

Directions: Write *m*, *d*, or *s* next to each picture whose name ends with /m/, /d/, or /s/ to complete the word.

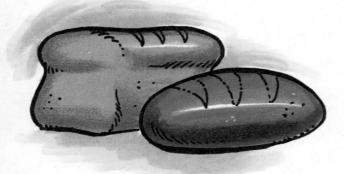

brea

dru

bu

Directions: Write *m*, *d*, or *s* next to each picture whose name ends with /*m*/, /*d*/, or /*s*/ to complete the word.

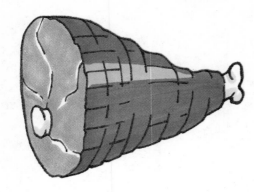

ha

ga

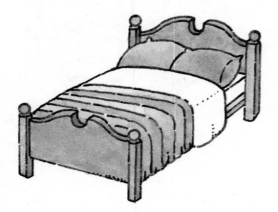

be

P p

P _____

p _____

_____

_____

Directions: Write the capital and small forms of the letter *Pp*. Write the letter *p* under the picture whose name begins with /p/.

UNIT 4   **The Wind • Lesson 10**   *What Happens When Wind Blows?*

Directions: Write the letter *p* under each picture whose name begins with /p/.

_____

- - - - - - - - - - - - - - - -

_____

_____

- - - - - - - - - - - - - - - -

_____

_____

- - - - - - - - - - - - - - - -

_____

_____

- - - - - - - - - - - - - - - -

_____

Directions: Write the letter *p* under each picture whose name ends with /p/, and write *m* under each picture whose name ends with /m/.

_____

- - - - - - - - - - - - - - - - - - - -

_____

- - - - - - - - - - - - - - - - - - - -

_____

- - - - - - - - - - - - - - - - - - - -

_____

- - - - - - - - - - - - - - - - - - - -

_____

- - - - - - - - - - - - - - - - - - - -

_____

- - - - - - - - - - - - - - - - - - - -

Directions: Write the letter *p* under each picture whose name ends with /p/, and write *m* under each picture whose name ends with /m/.

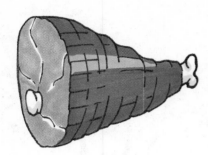

_____

- - - - - - - - - - - - - - -

_____

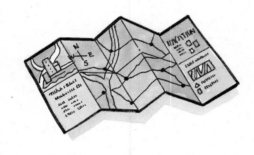

_____

- - - - - - - - - - - - - - -

_____

_____

- - - - - - - - - - - - - - -

_____

A a

A _____

a _____

Directions: Write the capital and small forms of the letter Aa. Write the letter a under the picture whose name has /a/ in it.

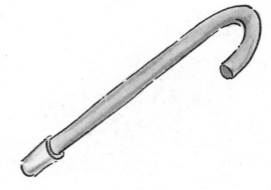

_____   _____

Directions: Write the letter a under each picture whose name has /a/ in it.

_____

_____

_____

_____

UNIT 4   The Wind • **Lesson 13** *Fine Art*

Directions: Circle the word with /a/ that names the picture. Then write the word.

bat   cat

_____

- -

_____

hat   pat

_____

- -

_____

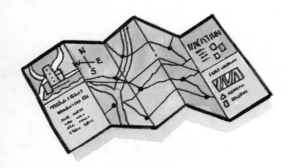

sap   map

_____

- -

_____

sad   pad

_____

- -

_____

Directions: Circle the word with / a / that names the picture. Then write the word.

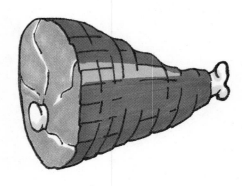

can   cap

_____

- - - - - - - - - - - - - - - - - - - -

_____

hat   ham

_____

- - - - - - - - - - - - - - - - - - - -

_____

ram   jam

_____

- - - - - - - - - - - - - - - - - - - -

_____

man   fan

_____

- - - - - - - - - - - - - - - - - - - -

_____

Directions: Write the capital and small forms of the letter *Hh*. Write the letter *h* under the picture whose name begins with /*h*/.

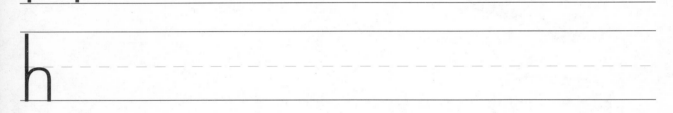

Directions: Write the letter *h* under each picture whose name begins with /h/.

_____

- - - - - - - - - - -

_____

_____

- - - - - - - - - - -

_____

_____

- - - - - - - - - - -

_____

_____

- - - - - - - - - - -

_____

UNIT 4   The Wind • **Lesson 15** *The Wind*

T t

Directions: Write the capital and small forms of the letter *Tt*. Write the letter *t* under the picture whose name begins with /t/.

T _____

t _____

_____

_____

_____

_____

_____

_____

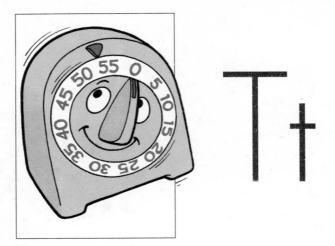

T t

T _____

t _____

_____

_____

Directions: Write the capital and small forms of the letter *Tt*. Write the letter *t* under the picture whose name ends with /t/.

Directions: Write the letter *t* under each picture whose name ends with /t/.

_____

_____

_____

_____

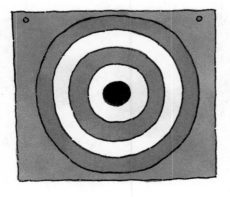

_____

_____

_____

_____

Directions: Write the capital and small forms of the letter Oo. Write the letter o under the picture whose name has /o/ in it.

Directions: Write the letter o under each picture whose name has /o/ in it.

_____

- - - - - - - - - - - - - - -

_____

_____

- - - - - - - - - - - - - - -

_____

_____

- - - - - - - - - - - - - - -

_____

_____

- - - - - - - - - - - - - - -

_____

Directions: Circle the word that names the picture. Then write the word.

lock   rock

_____

- - - - - - - - - - - -

_____

mop   tot

_____

- - - - - - - - - - - -

_____

hot   dog

_____

- - - - - - - - - - - -

_____

pot   drop

_____

- - - - - - - - - - - -

_____

UNIT 4 The Wind • **Lesson 18** *Wind Says Good Night*

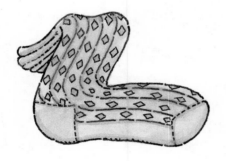

Nn

Directions: Write the capital and small forms of the letter *Nn*. Write the letter *n* under the picture whose name begins with /n/.

N

n

Directions: Write the letter *n* under each picture whose name begins with /n/.

_____   _____
- - - - - - - - - - - -   - - - - - - - - - - - -
_____   _____

_____   _____
- - - - - - - - - - - -   - - - - - - - - - - - -
_____   _____

UNIT 4 **The Wind • Lesson 20** *Unit Wrap-Up*

Directions: Write the letter *n* under each picture whose name ends with /n/.

Directions: Write the letter *n* under each picture whose name ends with /n/.

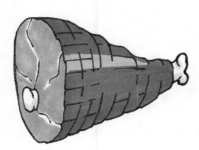

UNIT 5   **Stick to It • Lesson 2** *The Great Big Enormous Turnip*

Directions: Write the capital and small forms of the letter Ss. Write the letter s under the picture whose name begins with /s/.

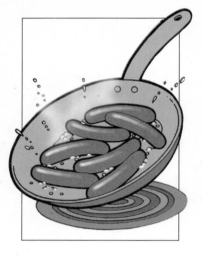

Ss

S _____

s _____

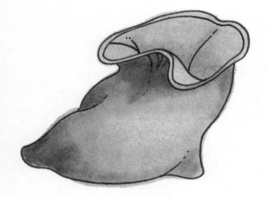

_____   _____

Directions: Write the letter s under each picture whose name ends with /s/.

_____

- - - - - - - - - - - - - - - - - -

_____

_____

- - - - - - - - - - - - - - - - - -

_____

UNIT 5   Stick to It • **Lesson 4** *The Great Big Enormous Turnip*

Directions: Write the capital and small forms of the letter *Mm*. Write the letter *m* under the picture whose name begins with /m/.

M

m

Directions: Write the letter *m* under each picture whose name ends with /m/.

_____

- - - - - - - - - - - -

_____

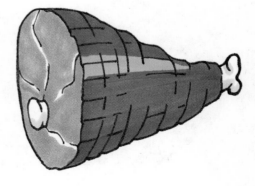

_____

- - - - - - - - - - - -

_____

UNIT 5   **Stick to It • Lesson 5** *The Great Big Enormous Turnip*

Aa

Directions: Write the capital and small forms of the letter Aa. Write the letter a under the picture whose name begins with /a/.

A _____

_____

a _____

_____

_____

_____

_____

Directions: Write the letter a under each picture whose name begins with /a/.

_____

- - - - - - - - - - - - - - - - -

_____

_____

- - - - - - - - - - - - - - - - -

_____

_____

- - - - - - - - - - - - - - - - -

_____

_____

- - - - - - - - - - - - - - - - -

_____

UNIT 5 **Stick to It • Lesson 6** *Tillie and the Wall*

A

a

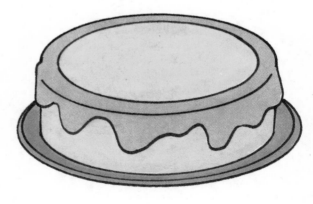

Identifying Short A • Sounds and Letters Skills

Directions: Write the capital and small forms of the letter Aa. Write the letter a under the picture whose name has /a/ in it.

Directions: Write the letter a under each picture whose name has /a/ in it.

_____

- - - - - - - - - - - - - - - - - - -

_____

_____

- - - - - - - - - - - - - - - - - - -

_____

_____

- - - - - - - - - - - - - - - - - - -

_____

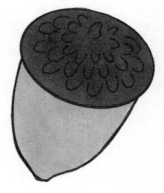

_____

- - - - - - - - - - - - - - - - - - -

_____

T t

Directions: Write the capital and small forms of the letter *Tt*. Write the letter *t* under the picture whose name begins with /t/.

T

t

UNIT 5   **Stick to It • Lesson 8** *Tillie and the Wall*

Directions: Write a capital *T* under each picture whose name begins with /t/ and write a small *t* under the picture that ends with /t/.

UNIT 5   **Stick to It • Lesson 12** *To Catch a Fish*

Hh

Directions: Write the capital and small forms of the letter *Hh*. Write the letter *h* under the picture whose name begins with /*h*/.

H _____

h _____

_____

_____

UNIT 5   **Stick to It • Lesson 12** *To Catch a Fish*

Directions: Write the letter *h* under each picture whose name begins with /h/.

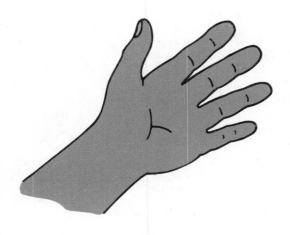

Pp

P _____

p _____

Directions: Write the capital and small forms of the letter *Pp*. Write the letter *p* under the picture whose name begins with /p/.

_____   _____

Directions: Write the letter *p* under each picture whose name ends with /p/.

Name _____

Name _____   Date _____

UNIT 5 **UNIT 5**   **Stick to It • Lesson 16** *Wanda's Roses*

Ii

I _____

i _____

_____

_____

76 UNIT 5 • Lesson 16   *Identifying Short I* • Sounds and Letters Skills

Directions: Write the capital and small forms of the letter *Ii*. Write the letter *i* under the picture whose name has /i/ in it.

Directions: Write the letter *i* under each picture whose name has /i/ in it.

_____

_ _ _ _ _ _ _ _ _ _ _ _ _

_____

_____

_ _ _ _ _ _ _ _ _ _ _ _ _

_____

_____

_ _ _ _ _ _ _ _ _ _ _ _ _

_____

_____

_ _ _ _ _ _ _ _ _ _ _ _ _

_____

L l

Directions: Write the capital and small forms of the letter *Ll*. Write the letter *l* under the picture whose name begins with /l/.

L

l

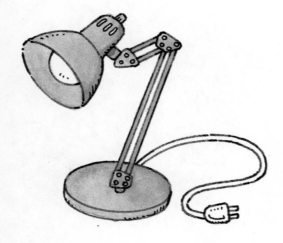

Directions: Write the letter *l* under each picture whose name begins with /l/.

UNIT 5   **Stick to It • Lesson 18** *Wanda's Roses*

Directions: Find and circle all the objects in the picture that end with /l/. Write the capital form of the letter *L l*.

Directions: Find and circle all the objects in the picture that end with /l/. Write the small form of the letter *Ll*.

_____

_____

N n

N

n

Directions: Write the capital and small forms of the letter *Nn*. Write the letter *n* under the picture whose name begins with /n/.

Directions: Write the letter *n* under each picture whose name begins with /n/.

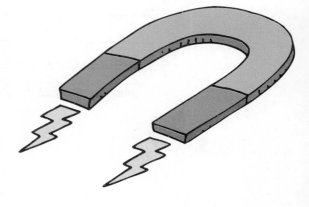

Directions: Circle all the items in the cart that end with /n/. Write the capital form of the letter *Nn*.

Directions: Circle all the items in the cart that end with /n/. Write the small form of the letter *Nn*.

UNIT 6   Red, White, and Blue • **Lesson 4** *Patriotism*

D d

D _____

d _____

_____   _____

_____   _____

Directions: Write the letter *d* under each picture whose name ends with /d/.

_____

- - - - - - - - - - - - - -

_____

_____

- - - - - - - - - - - - - -

_____

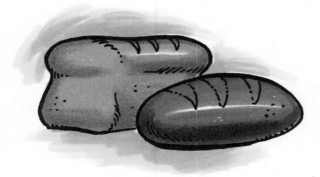

_____

- - - - - - - - - - - - - -

_____

_____

- - - - - - - - - - - - - -

_____

Directions: Write the capital and small forms of the letter Oo. Write the letter o under the picture whose name begins with /o/.

Directions: Write the letter o under each picture whose name has /o/ in it.

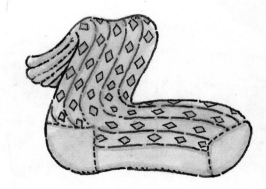

Bb

B

b

Directions: Write the capital and small forms of the letter Bb. Write the letter b under the picture whose name begins with /b/.

Directions: Write the letter *b* under each picture whose name begins with /b/.

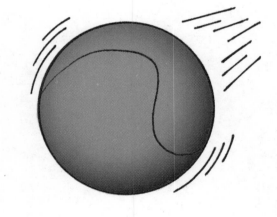

Directions: Circle all the pictures that end with /b/. Write the capital form of the letter Bb.

Directions: Circle all the pictures that end with /b/. Write the small form of the letter *Bb*.

Cc

C _____

c _____

Directions: Write the capital and small forms of the letter Cc. Write the letter c under the picture whose name begins with /k/.

Directions: Write the letter c under each picture whose name begins with /k/.

UNIT 6 Red, White, and Blue • **Lesson 12** *America the Beautiful!*

R r

R ‾ ‾ ‾ ‾ ‾ ‾ ‾ ‾ ‾ ‾ ‾ ‾

r ‾ ‾ ‾ ‾ ‾ ‾ ‾ ‾ ‾ ‾ ‾ ‾

Directions: Write the capital and small forms of the letter *Rr*. Write the letter *r* under the picture whose name begins with /r/.

UNIT 6 Red, White, and Blue • **Lesson 12** *America the Beautiful!*

Directions: Write the letter r under each picture whose name begins with /r/.

_____

_____

_____

_____

Directions: Write the letter r under each picture whose name ends with /r/.

Directions: Write the letter *r* under each picture whose name ends with /r/.

UNIT 6 Red, White, and Blue • **Lesson 15** *America the Beautiful!*

Uu

Directions: Write the capital and small forms of the letter *Uu*. Write the letter *u* under the picture whose name has / u/ in it.

U

u

Identifying Short U • Sounds and Letters Skills

Directions: Write the letter *u* under each picture whose name has /u/ in it.

_____

- - - - - - - - - - - - - - - - - - - -

_____

_____

- - - - - - - - - - - - - - - - - - - -

_____

_____

- - - - - - - - - - - - - - - - - - - -

_____

_____

- - - - - - - - - - - - - - - - - - - -

_____

Directions: Write the capital and small forms of the letter *Gg*. Write the letter *g* under the picture whose name begins with /g/.

Directions: Write the letter *g* under each picture whose name begins with /g/.

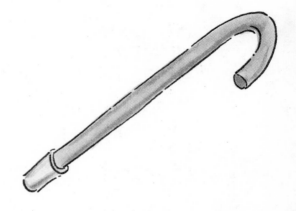

Directions: Circle the word with the final /g/ that names the picture. Then write the word.

pig   wig

_____

- - - - - - - - - - - - - - - - - - - -

_____

rug   bug

_____

- - - - - - - - - - - - - - - - - - - -

_____

pig   fig

_____

- - - - - - - - - - - - - - - - - - - -

_____

ladybug   hug

_____

- - - - - - - - - - - - - - - - - - - -

_____

UNIT 6 Red, White, and Blue • **Lesson 17** *The American Wei*

Directions: Circle the word with the final sound of /g/ that names the picture. Then write the word.

log   hog

_____

- - - - - - - - - - - - -

_____

egg   leg

_____

- - - - - - - - - - - - -

_____

hog   dog

_____

- - - - - - - - - - - - -

_____

bug   mug

_____

- - - - - - - - - - - - -

_____

Jj

Directions: Write the capital and small forms of the letter *Jj*. Write the letter *j* under the picture whose name begins with /j/.

J

j

Directions: Write the letter *j* under each picture whose name begins with /j/.

_____

- - - - - - - - - - - - - - - - - - -

_____

_____

- - - - - - - - - - - - - - - - - - -

_____

_____

- - - - - - - - - - - - - - - - - - -

_____

_____

- - - - - - - - - - - - - - - - - - -

_____

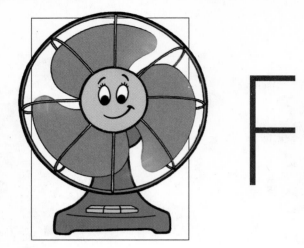

Ff

Directions: Write the capital and small forms of the letter *Ff*. Write the letter *f* under the picture whose name begins with /f/.

F

f

_____   _____

_____   _____

Directions: Write the letter f under each picture whose name begins with /f/.

_____

- - - - - - - - - - - - - - - -

_____

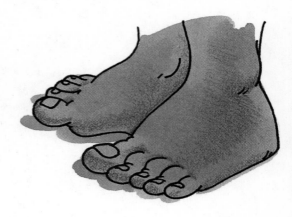

_____

- - - - - - - - - - - - - - - -

_____

_____

- - - - - - - - - - - - - - - -

_____

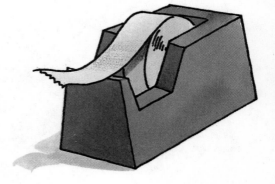

_____

- - - - - - - - - - - - - - - -

_____

Directions: Circle the objects in the picture whose names begin with /f/. Write the capital form of the letter *Ff*.

UNIT 7   Teamwork • **Lesson 2** *Team Time!*

Directions: Circle the objects in the picture whose names end with /f/.

Ee

E ‒‒‒‒‒‒‒‒‒‒‒‒‒‒‒‒‒‒‒‒‒‒‒‒‒‒‒‒‒‒‒‒‒‒

e ‒‒‒‒‒‒‒‒‒‒‒‒‒‒‒‒‒‒‒‒‒‒‒‒‒‒‒‒‒‒‒‒‒‒

_____   _____
‒‒‒‒‒‒‒‒‒‒‒‒‒‒‒‒‒‒‒‒‒‒‒   ‒‒‒‒‒‒‒‒‒‒‒‒‒‒‒‒‒‒‒‒‒‒‒
_____   _____

Directions: Write the capital and small forms of the letter Ee. Write the letter e under the picture whose name has /e/ in it.

Directions: Write the letter e under each picture whose name has /e/ in it.

_____

- - - - - - - - - - - - - - - -

_____

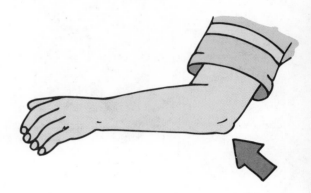

_____

- - - - - - - - - - - - - - - -

_____

_____

- - - - - - - - - - - - - - - -

_____

_____

- - - - - - - - - - - - - - - -

_____

Xx

X

x

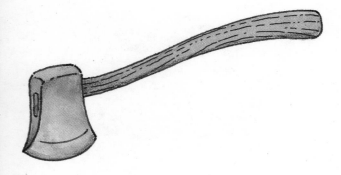

_____   _____

- - - - - - - - - - -   - - - - - - - - - - -

_____   _____

Directions: Write the capital and small forms of the letter Xx. Write the letter x under the picture whose name ends with /ks/.

UNIT 7 Teamwork • **Lesson 6** *Swimmy*

Directions: Write the letter x under each picture whose name ends with /ks/.

_____

- -

_____

_____

- -

_____

_____

- -

_____

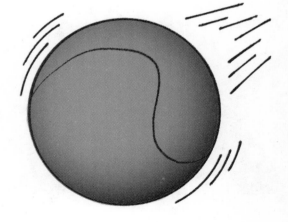

_____

- -

_____

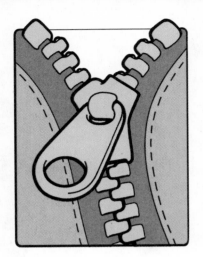

Zz

Directions: Write the capital and small forms of the letter Zz. Write the letter z under the picture whose name begins with /z/.

Z _____

_____

z _____

_____   _____

_____   _____

Directions: Write the letter z under each picture whose name ends with /z/.

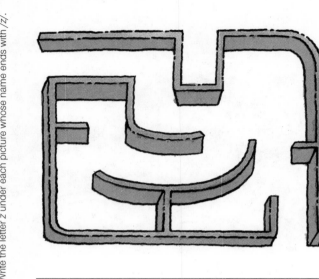

_____
- - - - - - - - - - - - - - -
_____

_____
- - - - - - - - - - - - - - -
_____

_____
- - - - - - - - - - - - - - -
_____

_____
- - - - - - - - - - - - - - -
_____

Directions: Tell the students to say each picture name. Then circle the letter in the name that makes the /z/ sound.

rose

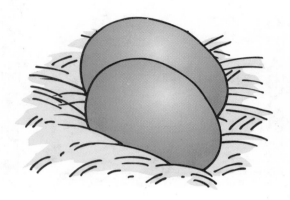

eggs

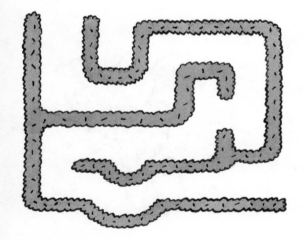

maze

blaze

Directions: Tell the students to say each picture name. Then circle the letter in the name that makes the /z/ sound.

prize

nose

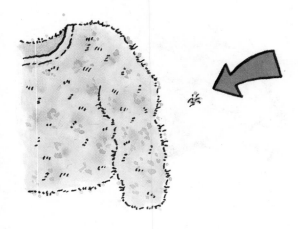

fuzz

wigs

Directions: Write the capital and small forms of the letter *Ww*. Write the letter *w* under the picture whose name begins with /w/.

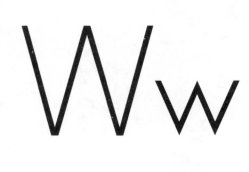

W _____

w _____

_____   _____

Directions: Write the letter *w* under each picture whose name begins with /w/.

_____

- - - - - - - - - - - - -

_____

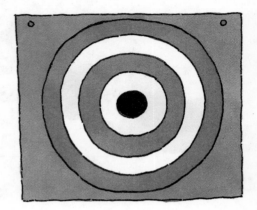

_____

- - - - - - - - - - - - -

_____

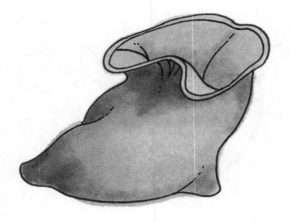

_____

- - - - - - - - - - - - -

_____

_____

- - - - - - - - - - - - -

_____

UNIT 7 Teamwork • **Lesson 12** *Cleaning Up the Block*

Kk

Directions: Write the capital and small forms of the letter Kk. Write the letter k under the picture whose name begins with /k/.

K _____

k _____

_____   _____

_____   _____

Directions: Write the letter *k* under each picture whose name begins with /k/.

Directions: Follow the maze and circle each stone with a picture whose name ends with /k/ to help the King find his bike. Write the capital form of the letter Kk.

Directions: Follow the maze and circle each stone with a picture whose name ends with /k/ to help the Queen find her book. Write the small form of the letter Kk.

Directions: Write the capital and small forms of the letter Qq. Write the letter q under the picture whose name begins with /kw/.

Q

q

_____   _____

Directions: Write the letter *q* under each picture whose name begins with /kw/.

UNIT 7   Teamwork • **Lesson 17**   *The Little Red Hen*

Y y

Y _____

y _____

Directions: Write the capital and small forms of the letter Yy. Write the letter y under the picture whose name begins with /y/.

_____ _____

_____ _____

UNIT 7 Teamwork • **Lesson 17** *The Little Red Hen*

Directions: Write the letter y under each picture whose name begins with /y/.

_____

- - - - - - - - - - - - - - -

_____

_____

- - - - - - - - - - - - - - -

_____

V v

Directions: Write the capital and small forms of the letter Vv. Write the letter v under the picture whose name begins with /v/.

V

v

Directions: Write a capital *V* under each picture whose name begins with /v/.
Write a small *v* under each picture that ends with /v/.

Directions: Blend and read each word. Then circle the word that completes the sentence.

_____

Look at the frog _____ .

hop

map

_____

He is on a _____ .

sled

sack

_____

The duck sits in the _____ .

tin

tub

Directions: Blend and read each word. Then circle the word that completes the sentence.

Pat can see the _____ .   beg   bug

Nan sat on the _____ .   hit   hat

Kim has milk in her _____ .   cot   cup

Directions: Blend and read each word. Then circle the word that completes the sentence.

_____   bun

Here is a _____ for the ham.   bin

_____   lit

Will has a bad _____.   leg

_____   tack

Mary put a _____ in the wall.   tick

Identifying Words • Sounds and Letters Skills

Directions: Blend and read each word. Then circle the word that completes the sentence.

_____

Here is a _____.

pin

pond

_____

Mike has a _____.

nap

cap

_____

Do you see the _____?

bug

bag

Directions: Blend and read each word. Then circle the word that completes the sentence.

_____

The lid is on the _____.

pot

mop

_____

Here is a dog in a _____.

wag

wig

_____

She likes to _____.

swim

jump

UNIT 8   By the Sea • **Lesson 7** *Humphrey the Lost Whale*

Directions: Blend and read each word. Then circle the word that completes the sentence.

_____ sink

I wash my hands in a _____. rink

_____ luck

The _____ was in the pond. duck

_____ bat

Dave has a new _____. mat

See the ant _____.

zigzag

limp

Bees like to _____.

sit

buzz

Mom has a big _____.

trip

van

Directions: Blend and read each word. Then circle the word that completes the sentence.

_____

The _____ is by the farm.

brain

train

_____ lake

We want to sit by the _____. bake

_____

I see a _____!

skunk

trunk

Sounds and Letters Skills • *Identifying Words*   UNIT 8 • Lesson 9   **139**

_____

steps

The man _____.

slips

_____

pan

The egg is in the _____.

vat

_____

hand

Meg can pitch a _____.

ball

_____   milk

Stan likes to drink _____.   silk

_____   stuff

John ripped his _____.   cuff

_____   sock

We will _____ the door.   lock

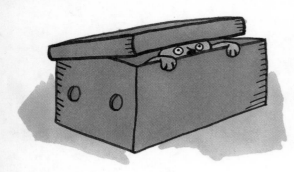

_____ fox

What is in the _____? box

_____ socks

My cat is on my _____. bike

_____ cub

The bear hugs her _____. pup

Directions: Blend and read each word. Then circle the word that completes the sentence.

Directions: Blend and read each word. Then circle the word that completes the sentence.

The baby is in the _____ .   bib

crib

stump

The _____ is in her yard.   jump

vet

The _____ looked at the dog. bet

Directions: Blend and read each word. Then circle the word that completes the sentence.

_____

Sue has on a _____.

cape

cap

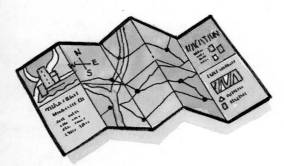

_____

Let's look at the _____.

mat

map

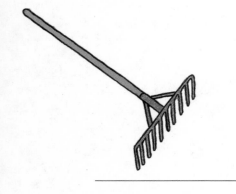

_____

Is the _____ in the shed?

rake

wake

UNIT 8   By the Sea • **Lesson 17** *Hello Ocean*

Directions: Blend and read each word. Then circle the word that completes the sentence.

_____

Dad likes to _____.

tape

tap

_____

The hen sits on her _____.

nose

nest

kite

quilt

_____

Look at my _____.